Classic Ballads
FOR TROMBONE

T0085419

To access audio visit:
www.halleonard.com/mylibrary
Enter Code
3709-3393-7641-3371

ISBN 978-0-99163-477-4

Music Minus One

Exclusively Distributed By

Hal•Leonard®

Contact Us:
Hal Leonard
7777 West Bluemound Road
Milwaukee, WI 53213
Email: info@halleonard.com

In Europe contact:
Hal Leonard Europe Limited
42 Wigmore Street
Marylebone, London, W1U 2RN
Email: info@halleonardeurope.com

In Australia contact:
Hal Leonard Australia Pty. Ltd.
4 Lentara Court
Cheltenham, Victoria, 3192 Australia
Email: info@halleonard.com.au

Stardust

Words and Music by
Mitchell Parish and Hoagy Carmichael

MMO 3943

4

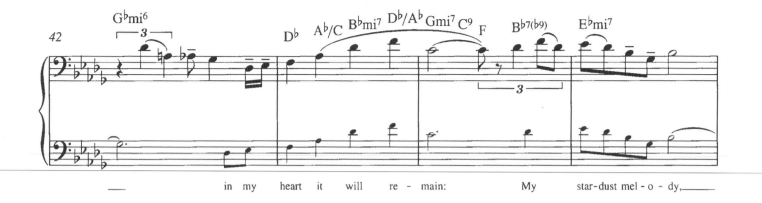

in my heart it will re - main: My star-dust mel - o - dy,____

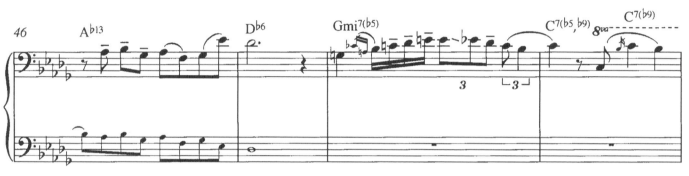

____ the mem-o - ry of love's re - frain.

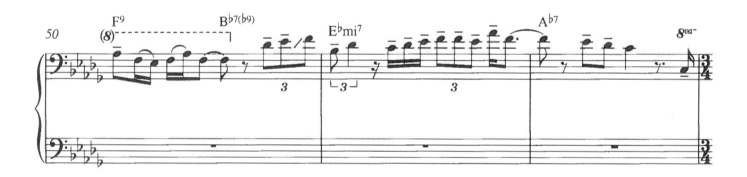

Yesterdays

Words and Music by
Otto Harbach and Jerome Kern

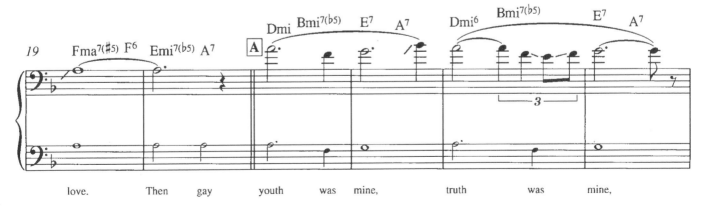

MMO 3943

joy - ous, free and flam - ing life, for - sooth, was mine, sad am

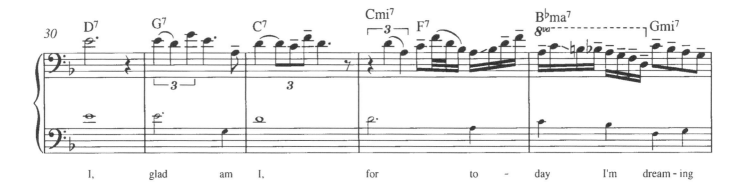

I, glad am I, for to - day I'm dream - ing

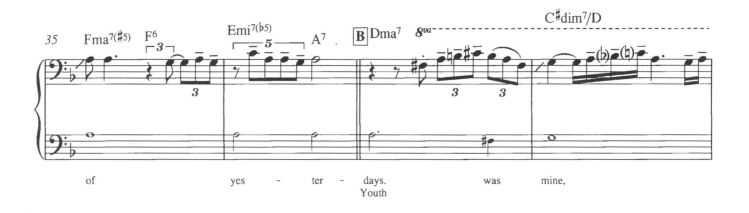

of yes - ter - days. was mine,
Youth

truth was mine, joy-ous, free and flam-ing life, for-sooth, was mine,

sad   am   I,   glad   am   I,   for   to -

day   I'm   dream – ing   of   yes – ter – days.

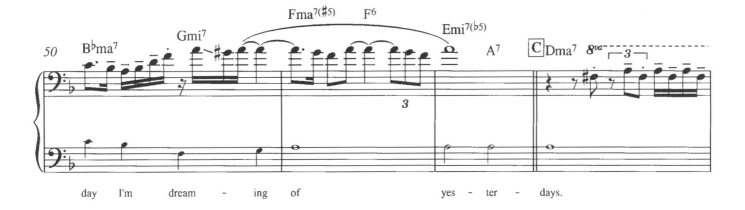

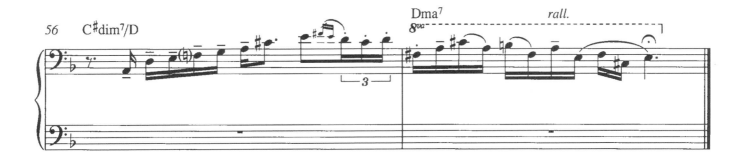

Embraceable You

Words and Music by
Ira Gershwin and George Gershwin

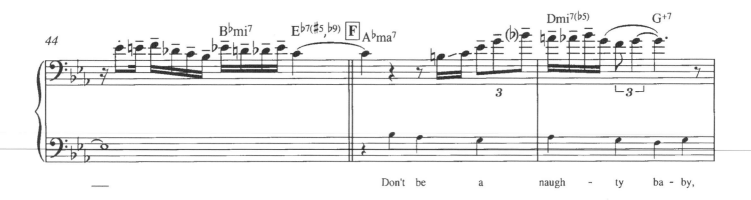

Don't be a naugh - ty ba - by,

come to pa - pa, come to pa - pa, do!   My sweet em -

brace - a - ble   you!

What's New?

Words and Music by
Johnny Burke and Bob Haggart

MMO 3943

of - fer your hand,   I un - der - stand.___ A - dieu,

par-don my ask-ing what's new?___   Of course you   could - n't

know   I have-n't changed, I still love you so.___

Blue Moon

Words and Music by
Lorenz Hart and Richard Rodgers

bod - y whis - per, "Please a - dore me"_____ And when I looked, the moon had turned to

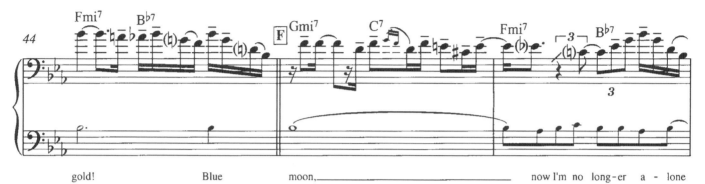

gold! Blue moon,_____ now I'm no long-er a - lone

_____ with-out a dream in my heart,_____with-out a love of my own.___

Smoke Gets In Your Eyes

Words and Music by
Otto Harbach and Jerome Kern

MMO 3943

So I chaffed them and I gay - ly laughed, to think they could doubt my love.

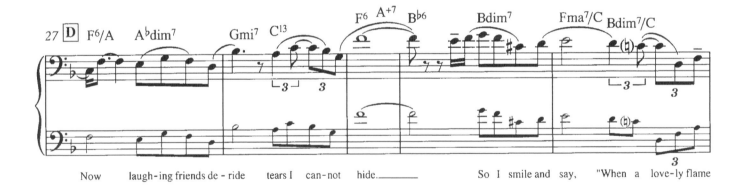

Yet to - day,— my love has flown a - way,— I am with - out my love.

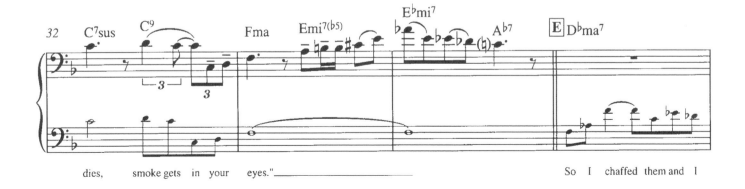

Now laugh-ing friends de - ride tears I can-not hide.⎯⎯⎯ So I smile and say, "When a love-ly flame

dies, smoke gets in your eyes."⎯⎯⎯⎯⎯⎯ So I chaffed them and I

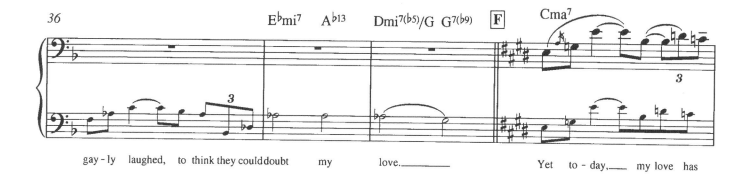

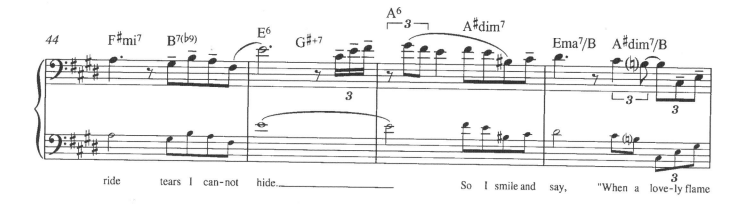

Memories of You

Words and Music by
Andy Razof and Eubie Blake

mem - o - ries of you. How I wish I could for-get those hap-py yes-ter-

years that have left a ro - sa - ry of tears.

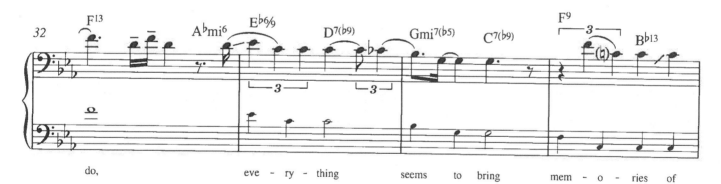

Your face beams in my dreams 'spite of all I

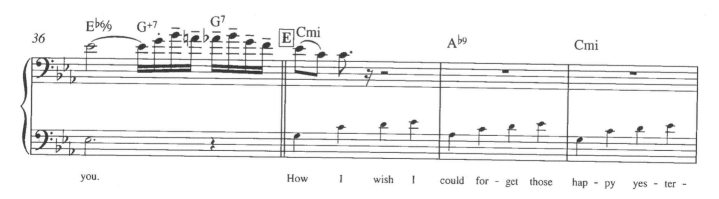

do, eve - ry - thing seems to bring mem - o - ries of

you. How I wish I could for-get those hap-py yes-ter-

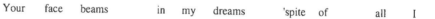

years   that have left a   ro - sa - ry of tears._____

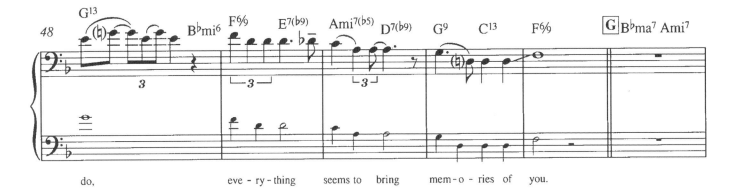

____   Your   face beams   in my dreams 'spite of all I

do,   eve - ry - thing seems to bring mem - o - ries of you.

Laura

Words and Music by
Johnny Mercer and David Raksin

MMO 3943

She gave___ your ver - y first kiss to you.___ That was Lau - ra,___

___ but she's on - ly a dream. And you see Lau - ra___ on the train that is

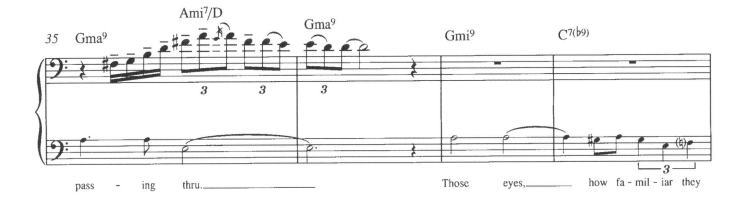

pass - ing thru.___ Those eyes,___ how fa - mil - iar they

seem.___ She gave___ your ver - y first kiss to you.___

That was Lau - ra,_____ but she's on - ly a dream.

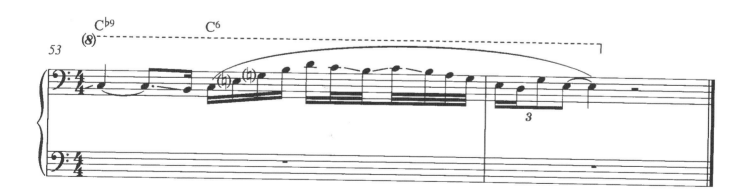

Can't Help Lovin' That Man of Mine

Words and Music by
Oscar Hammerstein II and Jerome Kern

back dat day is fine,_____ the sune will shine.

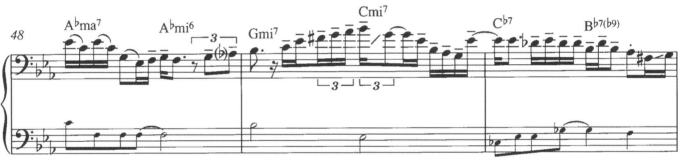

He can come home_____ as late as can be,_____ home with-out him_____ ain't

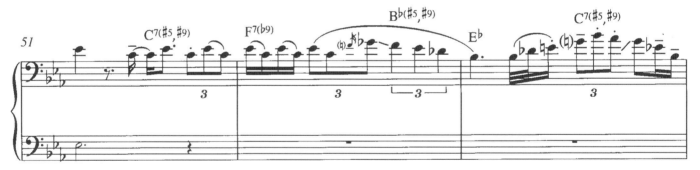

no home to me,_____ can't help lov-in' that man_____ of

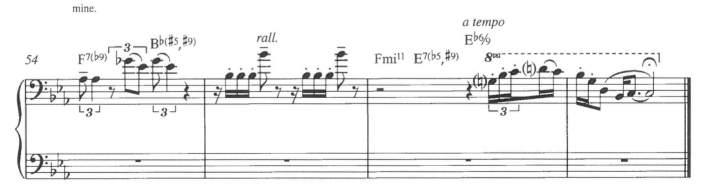

mine.

Willow Weep For Me

Words and Music by
Ann Ronell

Oh, wil-low weep for me,—

wil-low weep for me,— bend your branch-es green— a-long the stream— that runs to sea.—

Lis-ten to my plea, lis-ten wil-low and weep for— me.—

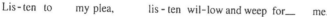

Gone my lov-er's dream, love-ly sum-mer dream, gone and left me here— to weep my tears— in-to the stream;

sad as I can be, hear me wil-low and weep for— me.—

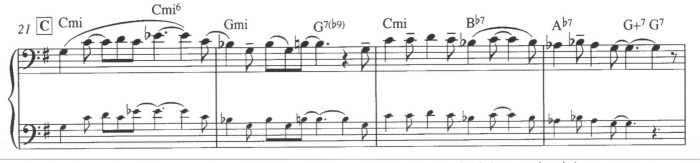

Whis-per to the wind_____ and say that love has sinned_____ to leave my heart a-break-ing____ and mak-ing a moan.

Mur - mur to the night_____ to hide her star-ry light,_____ so none will find me sigh - ing____ and

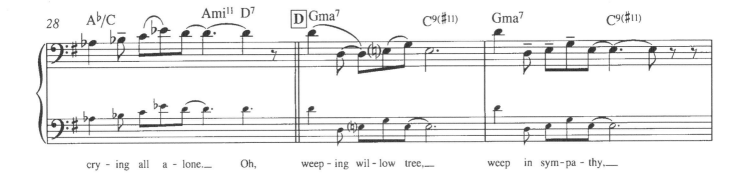

cry - ing all a - lone.____ Oh, weep-ing wil-low tree,___ weep in sym-pa-thy,___

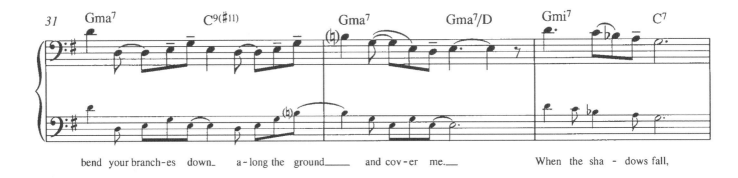

bend your branch-es down____ a-long the ground_____ and cov-er me.____ When the sha - dows fall,

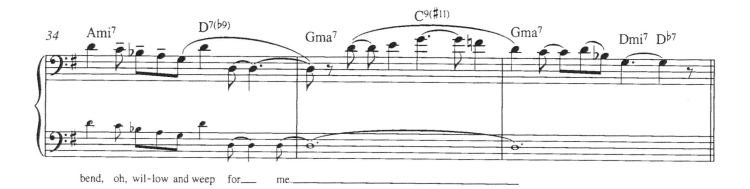

bend, oh, wil-low and weep for___ me._____

Whis-per to the wind_____ and say that love has sinned___ to leave my heart a-break-ing__ and mak-ing a moan.

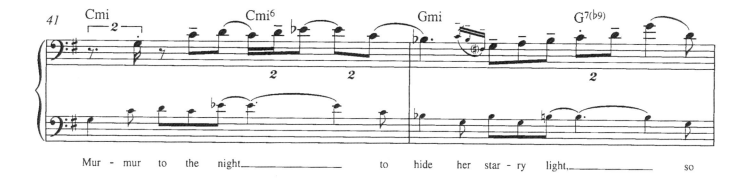

Mur - mur to the night_____ to hide her star - ry light,_____ so

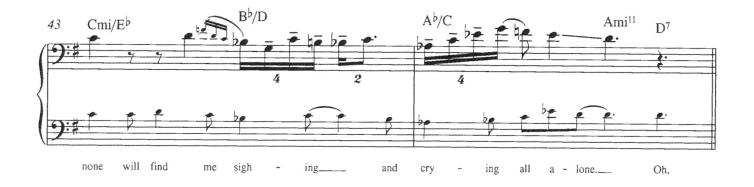

none will find me sigh - ing_____ and cry - ing all a - lone.___ Oh,

weep - ing wil - low tree,____   weep   in   sym - pa - thy,____

bend   your branch-es down   a - long   the   ground____ and cov-er me.____   When the sha-dows fall,

bend, oh, wil-low and weep   for__   me._____